EVERYDAY
Macramé

≫ 10 STYLISH PROJECTS FOR YOUR HOME ≪

Justine Vasquez

becker&mayer!
BOOK PRODUCERS

becker&mayer!
BOOK PRODUCERS

Produced by becker&mayer!, LLC.
11120 NE 33rd Place, Suite 101
Bellevue, WA 98004
www.beckermayer.com

If you have questions or comments about this product, please visit
www.beckermayer.com/customerservice.html and click on the
Customer Service Request Form.

Written by Justine Vasquez
Design by Megan Sugiyama
Editorial by Nancy W. Cortelyou
Photography by Joseph Lambert
Production coordination by Cindy Curren
Product sourcing by Jen Matasich

Printed, manufactured, and assembled in Shenzhen, China, 07/2016

10 9 8 7 6 5 4 3 2 1

ISBN: 978-1-60380-385-4
UPC: 834509005002

Project #15677
Project #15678

Contents

Welcome to Everyday Macramé!

In this book, you will find a fresh, modern perspective on the classic craft. You will learn the basics and essentials of macramé, while being guided through ten unique projects. When you think of macramé, you may think of plant hangers from the 1970s. However, in this book, you will discover bright colors, new materials, clean lines, and a whole new approach to traditional macramé.

Macramé is such a versatile craft because you can create something even if you only know a few knots. You can add and build upon each piece. And if you mess up, you just undo the knot and try again! There's plenty of room for mistakes and a forgiving learning curve here.

Whether you are looking to make a simple plant hanger, a stunning wall hanging, or a new bag, you will find something that suits you in this book!

What's in the Box

(to make the Mini Plant Hanger and the Mini Wall Hanging):

- 150 feet of cord
- 13-inch wooden dowel
- 10 beads

Additional Materials Needed

(to complete all projects):

- Cord (variety of types and colors)
- Wooden dowels: (1) 8-inch
- Copper pipes: (3) 10-inch
- Wood piece: (1) 12-by-5½-by-¾ inches
- Metal rings: (1) 8-inch metal ring; (1) 2-inch metal ring
- Lamp shade frame
- Single socket pendant light
- Light bulb
- Needle and thread
- Beads (variety of sizes and colors) *Beads need to be just large enough to fit the cords through.*
- Fabric glue
- Wall hook or swivel, or even a nail in the wall

Optional Materials:

- Pins (to help hold cord in place as you work)
- Tape (to help hold cord in place as you work)
- Working board (to help hold cord in place as you work)
- Lighter (to seal the ends of polyolefin cord to prevent fraying)
- Fabric dye (to dip dye projects like the Mini Wall Hanging and the Owl.)

Techniques

There are a few knots that are used in most of the macramé projects. See the Knot Know-How section (turn the page) to start mastering these essential techniques right away as well as some varations.

- Overhand knot
- Lark's head knot
- Gathering knot
- Square knot
- Double half hitch knot

There are a few terms that are helpful to know when making macramé pieces.

- **Working cord:** The cord(s) you are using to complete the knots.
- **Holding cord:** The cord(s) that stays in place to hold the knots made by the working cords. (The holding cord acts as a filler cord, running through the center of the knots.)
- **Sinnet:** A group of five or more of the same knot.
- **Seal:** If you're using polyolefin cord, sealing the ends with a lighter will help keep the cords from fraying and unraveling.

Tips

- When working on a project that requires a lot of knot work, seal the ends of the cord (if you are using polyolefin cord with a lighter, or use tape). Clean cords are easier to work with, whether you are making knots or threading beads.

- When making macramé pieces that hang, such as plant hangers or wall hangings, attach the working cords to a hook or swivel.

- When making macramé pieces that lay flat, such as coasters, bags, or rugs, use pins or tape to keep the cords in place on a table or working board.

- Be precise when measuring out and cutting your cord to help keep your work consistent.

Knot Know-How:

Instructions for all of the KNOTS used in this book can be found here for reference:

Fig. A

Fig. B

Overhand Knot

1. Cut a strand of cord.

2. Take the right end of the cord and loop over the left end. (**Fig. A**)

3. Pull the right end up through the loop and tighten. (**Fig. B**)

Lark's Head Knot

1. Fold a strand of cord in half.

2. Hold the folded working cord behind and slightly above your holding cord (or dowel or ring). (Fig. A)

3. Fold the working cord over the holding cord, then bring the loose ends of the folded cord through the loop and tighten. (Figs. B–D)

Fig. B

Fig. C

Fig. D

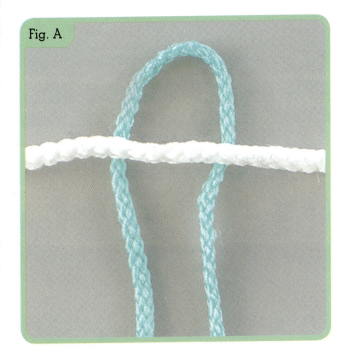

Fig. A

Fig. A

Fig. B

Fig. C

Fig. D

Fig. E

Gathering Knot

1. Cut as many strands of cord as you need for your project and thread all of them through a ring, keeping the cords centered on the ring. (Fig. A)

2. Cut another cord about 20 inches long.

3. Hold the left end of the 20-inch cord just above the ring and fold the cord about 3 inches down from the ring. (Fig. B) The right end of the cord should be left long in order to wrap around the gathered cords. (The folded cord will create a loop (Fig. C), which you will pull the right end of the cord through. (Fig. D)

4. Take the right end of the cord and start wrapping around the gathered cords including the top portion of the working cord.

5. Wrap around the cords six to eight times and thread the end through the loop that you created in Step 3. (Fig. E)

6. Take the end of the left working cord that is sticking out of the top of the gathering knot, and pull to tighten. Trim the ends.

Spiral Knot

1. Make a **HALF KNOT,** and then continue making half knots to create a spiral effect. (A spiral knot is best made with at least 10 knots.) **(Figs. A–C)**

Gathering Double Half Hitch Knot

1. Secure a dowel or a holding cord.

2. Secure four strands of cord using a **LARK'S HEAD KNOT**, for a total of eight strands.

3. Using the outer right cord as your holding cord, tie a **DOUBLE HALF HITCH KNOT** onto the holding cord with the cord directly next to it. Instead of dropping it and going to the next cord, hold onto it and take the next cord in your hand as well. You will havve two working cords in your hands.

4. Tie a **DOUBLE HALF HITCH KNOT** with both cords. Keep adding a cord as you go, gathering them up and tying the double half hitch knots until you are at the end of the left side.

Fig. A

Fig. B

Fig. C

Fig. A

Fig. B

Fig. C

Alternating Half Hitch Knot

1. Secure two strands of cord using a **LARK'S HEAD KNOT** or **OVERHAND KNOT**. (Fig. A) The two center cords will be the holding cords, and the left and right cords will be the working cords.

2. Take the left cord and thread it over and back under the holding cords, and then over itself. (Fig. B)

3. Take the right cord and repeat this process going in the opposite direction. (Fig. C)

4. Continue alternating between the left and right sides, keeping the knots close together. Make sure to follow the pattern over, under, and over again.

Square Knot

1. Secure two strands of cord using a **LARK'S HEAD KNOT**. Then, take the left working cord over the two center cords and then under the right cord. The left cord should take the shape of a "C". (**Fig. A**)

2. Take the right cord under the two center cords and up through the center of the "C" and over the left working cord. (**Fig. B**)

3. Pull both cords to tighten and secure. (**Fig. C**)

4. On the opposite side, take the right working cord over the two center cords and then under the left cord. This will be your backwards "C". (**Fig. D**)

5. Take the left cord under the two center cords and up through the backwards "C" and over the right working cord.

6. Pull and tighten. (**Fig. E**)

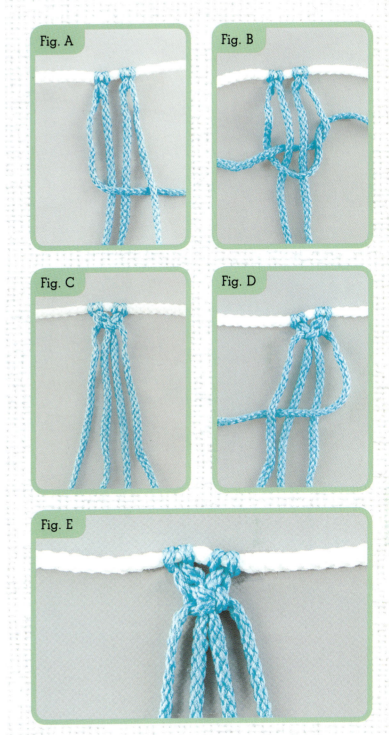

Fig. A
Fig. B
Fig. C
Fig. D
Fig. E

Fig. A

Fig. B

Fig. C

Fig. D

Alternating Square Knot

1. Secure four sets of cord using a **LARK'S HEAD KNOT**. (Fig. A)

2. Divide the eight hanging cords into two groups of four.

3. Take the left group of cords and make a **SQUARE KNOT**. Then, take the right group of cords and make another **SQUARE KNOT**. (Fig. B)

4. Take the middle four cords and make a **SQUARE KNOT**. (There should be two cords still hanging on the far left and two cords on the far right.)

5. Repeat Step 3, making a **SQUARE KNOT** using the left four cords and the right four cords. (Fig. C)

6. Repeat to keep making alternating square knots. (Fig. D)

Square Knot Sinnet

1. Repeat the **SQUARE KNOT** five or more times in a row to make a sinnet. (Fig. A)

A sinnet can actually be made with any type of knot, by making a minimum of five of the same knot in a row.

Fig. A

Double Half Hitch Knot

1. Secure a holding cord with tape to a table or use a working board.

2. Take a strand of cord and secure the top end.

3. Take the other end of the cord and thread it under the holding cord, then over the holding cord, and back down under the holding cord and down over itself. Tighten. (Fig. A)

4. Repeat Step 3 and tighten. (Fig. B)

Fig. A

Fig. B

Fig. A

Fig. B

Fig. C

Josephine Knot

1. Secure two sets of cords using a **LARK'S HEAD KNOT** or **OVERHAND KNOT**. You will have four working cords, two cords on the left and two cords on the right. (**Fig. A**)

2. Take the left group of working cords and make a loop. The loop should be on the right, while the trailing ends should hang to the left. (**Fig. B**) The end of the cords will go under itself.

3. Take the right group of cords and go over the loop and under the ends of the left group. (**Figs. C & D**)

4. Continue taking the right set of cords over the left cords, under the cords at the top of the first loop, over itself, and under the bottom of the first loop. There will be two loops, with the ends of the cords hanging down. (**Fig. E**)

5. Adjust and tighten. (**Fig. F**)

Half Knot

1. Secure two strands of cord using a **LARK'S HEAD KNOT**.

2. Take the left working cord over the two center cords and then under the right cord. The left cord will take the shape of a "C".

3. Take the right cord under the two center cords and up through the center of the "C" and over the left working cord.

4. Pull both cords to tighten and secure.

Trivet Knot

1. See the coaster project on page 36. A finished coaster is an example of a trivet knot.

Fig. D

Fig. E

Fig. F

MINI PLANT HANGER

(will hold pots up to about 6 inches in diameter)

MATERIALS:

- 26 feet of cord
- Wall hook or swivel
- 4 beads

KNOTS TO KNOW:

- Gathering knot
- Overhand knot

INSTRUCTIONS:

1. Cut four 70-inch strands of cord.

2. Using a wall hook or swivel, fold the four strands of cord in half and place the cord over the hook to create eight hanging strands of cord.

3. Cut a 20-inch strand of cord and tie a **GATHERING KNOT** about 1½ inches down from the hook around all eight strands. (This creates a loop at the top, from which you will hang the finished plant hanger.)

4. Take two strands of cord and thread them both through one bead.

5. Tie an **OVERHAND KNOT** 8 inches down. Repeat with the other six strands, in pairs. (Fig. A)

6. Another 4 inches down, take two sets of cord and choose the right cord from the left group and the left cord from the right group, and make an overhand knot. (Figs. B & C)

7. Repeat three more times with the remaining sets of cord.

8. Tie a second gathering knot about 3½ inches down from the overhand knots that were made in Steps 6 and 7.

9. Cut the ends of the hanging cords to your desired length.

10. Tuck in a small plant like a succulent and hang your handiwork for all to see!

Fig. A

Fig. B

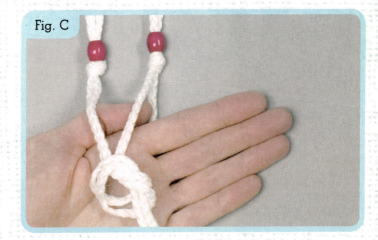
Fig. C

MINI WALL HANGING

MATERIALS:

- 107 feet of cord
- 13-inch wooden dowel
- Hook or swivel
- 6 beads
- Fabric dye

KNOTS TO KNOW:

- Lark's head knot
- Square knot
- Alternating square knot
- Josephine knot

INSTRUCTIONS:

1. Cut one 24-inch strand of cord and tie both ends on the dowel. Use this cord to hang onto a hook.

2. Cut fourteen 90-inch strands of cord.

3. Fold each strand in half and tie onto the wooden dowel using **LARK'S HEAD KNOTS**. Be sure the cords are all evenly spaced from each other.

4. Make two **SQUARE KNOTS** with each pairing of cords along the first row. There will be seven sets.

5. Make five rows of **ALTERNATING SQUARE KNOTS**.

6. Thread one bead through the holding cords of the six inner sets of cord. There will be two cords left hanging on each side of the wall hanging.

7. Use the outer working cords and make a square knot under each bead.

8. For the next row, use two cords from each set to make a **JOSEPHINE KNOT**. Use two right cords from the left set, and two left cords from the right set until you have a row of five Josephine knots. (Figs. A–F)

9. Continue with six more rows of **ALTERNATING SQUARE KNOTS**.

10. The sixth row will have six square knots. From there, continue but take away a knot on each row. The next row will only have five square knots. The row after that will have four, and so on. The last row will only have one square knot.

11. Cut the ends, either straight across or at varied lengths.

12. If desired, dye the ends by dipping them in fabric dye. Be sure to follow the manufacturer's directions.

Fig. A

Fig. B

Fig. C

Fig. D

Fig. E

Fig. F

LONG PLANT HANGER

(will hold pots up to about 12 inches in diameter)

MATERIALS:

- 102 feet of cord
- Metal ring

KNOTS TO KNOW:

- Gathering knot
- Overhand knot
- Square knot sinnet
- Square knot
- Alternating half hitch knot

INSTRUCTIONS:

1. Cut eight 150-inch strands of cord.

2. Thread cords through a metal ring, making sure the ends meet and the cord ends are even.

3. Cut one 20-inch strand of cord and use this to make a **GATHERING KNOT** around all sixteen cords.

4. If there are any ends sticking out from the gathering knot, trim and seal them.

5. Separate the cords into four groups of four. Tie each group into a loose **OVERHAND KNOT**, without pulling the cords all the way through the loop, to keep them together and separate from the group you're working on.

6. Grab one group of four cords. Remove the overhand knot, then make a sinnet of five **SQUARE KNOTS**.

7. The two middle cords (holding cords) will now be your working cords. Take these two cords and make two square knots 2 inches down, using the former working cords as your holding cords. It should look as if the middle cords are crossing over. (Figs. A & B)

8. Make five **ALTERNATING HALF HITCH KNOTS**. (Figs C–F)

9. Now make two **SQUARE KNOTS**.

10. Once again, take your middle holding cords and make two **SQUARE KNOTS** 2 inches down.

Fig. A

Fig. B

Fig. C

Fig.D

11. Make five **ALTERNATING HALF HITCH KNOTS** and two more **SQUARE KNOTS**.

12. Cross the cords one last time 2 inches down and make another sinnet of five **SQUARE KNOTS**.

13. Repeat Steps 6 through 12 with the other three groups of cord.

14. Once all four sides have been completed, measure down about 5½ inches and take two of the finished groups, totaling eight strands of cord.

15. Use the two right cords on the left group and the two left cords on the right group. This will give you four cords to use to connect the two sides. The two outer cords will be your working cords.

16. Make two **SQUARE KNOTS**.

17. Repeat Steps 15 and 16 three more times to connect the remaining sides.

18. Make a **GATHERING KNOT** another 5½ inches down. You can adjust the height of the gathering knot to accommodate a larger or smaller pot.

There are countless ways to make plant hangers and there's no pressure about messing up—mistakes just add to their uniqueness. For brown thumbs, it also might inspire you to keep your plants alive so you can have something to display in your handcrafted plant hangers!

A sinnet can actually be made with any type of knot, by making a minimum of five of the same knot in a row.

Fig. E

Fig. F

COPPER WALL HANGING

MATERIALS:

- 54 feet of cord
- Three 10-inch copper pipes

KNOTS TO KNOW:

- Gathering knot
- Lark's head knot
- Square knot
- Alternating square knot
- Double half hitch knot
- Spiral knot

INSTRUCTIONS:

1. Cut one 70-inch strand of cord and thread it through your three pieces of copper piping twice to form a triangle.

2. Bring the ends of the cord over a hook and tie a GATHERING KNOT around the cords, about 1½ inches down, to create a loop.

3. Cut extra cord and seal (this will be the loop to hang the wall hanging).

4. Cut twelve 48-inch strands of cord.

5. Fold each cord in half and tie onto the bottom horizontal piece of copper pipe using LARK'S HEAD KNOTS.

6. Make a row of SQUARE KNOTS.

7. Continue making rows of ALTERNATING SQUARE KNOTS until you have five rows of square knots.

8. Bring the outer left cord, which will be the holding cord, over the working cords horizontally. It may be helpful to secure the right end of this holding cord. (Fig. A)

9. Using the cord directly next to the holding cord, tie a DOUBLE HALF HITCH KNOT onto the holding cord. Continue tying double half hitch knots until you have reached the last cord on the outer right side. (Figs. B & C)

10. Divide the cords into six sets of four. With the first set of cords, tie a sinnet of six SQUARE KNOTS.

11. With the second set of cords, tie a sinnet of twelve SPIRAL KNOTS.

Fig. A

Fig. B

Fig. C

12. Repeat Steps 10 and 11 with the four remaining sets of cord, following the pattern of square knots, then spiral knots, square knots, and spiral knots.

13. Repeat Steps 8 and 9.

14. Tie a row of **SQUARE KNOTS** about 1 inch down.

15. Continue making rows of **ALTERNATING SQUARE KNOTS**, subtracting one with each row, until you only have one square knot left on the sixth row. Keep the spacing even between each row.

16. Make a **SQUARE KNOT** using the four outer left cords, about 6 inches down from the top square knot.

17. Make a second **SQUARE KNOT** about 1 inch farther down using the right cord from the set of cords you just used and the next three cords. Repeat twice to get to the center knot.

18. Repeat Steps 16 and 17 on the right side, starting with the four outer right cords. Cut ends to your desired length.

Copper can make the macramé pieces more sophisticated and edgy. Try using smaller one-inch pieces of copper piping to add to your plant hangers!

LAMP SHADE

MATERIALS:

- 71 feet of cord*
- One 8-inch lamp shade frame
- One 8-inch metal ring
- Single socket pendant light
- Light bulb

KNOTS TO KNOW:

- Lark's head knot
- Square knot
- Alternating square knot
- Double half hitch knot

* If you would like to use two different colors, cut fifteen 25-inch strands of one color, and fifteen 25-inch strands plus two 50-inch strands in another color, totaling 31 feet for color one and 40 feet for color two.

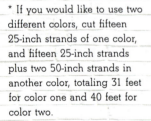

INSTRUCTIONS:

1. Cut thirty 25-inch strands of cord and two 50-inch strands of cord.

2. Fold each 25-inch strand of cord in half and tie onto the lamp shade frame using LARK'S HEAD KNOTS, keeping them spaced evenly from each other. If using two different colors, alternate the colors in your desired pattern. (Fig. A)

3. Using two sets of cords, make a SQUARE KNOT 1½ inches down from the top of frame. Continue to complete a row of square knots. (Figs. B–D)

4. Tie four rows of ALTERNATING SQUARE KNOTS until the pattern is about 6 inches long. (Figs. E & F)

5. Tie each individual cord onto the metal ring using DOUBLE HALF HITCH KNOTS. The cord will now be secured to the ring, keeping it connected to the frame, forming a lamp shade.

6. To cover the frame's exposed metal, use one 50-inch strand of cord and tie it onto the frame using a DOUBLE HALF HITCH KNOT. Continue making double half hitch knots along the entire frame until you've reached the other end of the cord. Tie the two ends together, cut and seal.

7. Repeat Step 6 for the ring. The ends of the cords will be hanging down. You may leave them hanging or cut them to your desired length.

8. Feed the end of the pendant light fixture through the top of the hole in the lamp shade frame and screw in a light bulb.

9. Hang up, plug in, and enjoy your macramé-crafted light fixture!

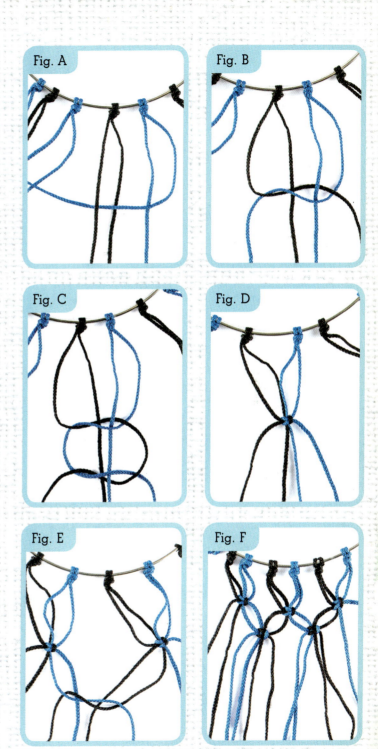

Fig. A

Fig. B

Fig. C

Fig. D

Fig. E

Fig. F

Project 6

THROW RUG

(about 2½ by 1½ feet)

MATERIALS:

- 200 feet white cord
- 72 feet navy cord

KNOTS TO KNOW:

- Double half hitch knot
- Square knot
- Square knot sinnet
- Alternating square knot

Choose any color or combination of colors you like for this project. Directions are specific to the two-color rug pictured.

INSTRUCTIONS:

1. Cut thirty-two 6-foot strands of white cord, four 2-foot strands of white cord, and twelve 6-foot strands of navy cord.

2. Lay out the forty-four of the six-foot pieces of cord flat, starting with eight white strands, then four navy strands, eight white, four navy, eight white, four navy, and eight white.

3. Lay one 2-foot-strand of white cord across all forty-four pieces horizontally, about 3 inches down from one of the ends. This cord is going to be the holding cord, which all the working cords will be secured to.

4. Secure all forty-four working cords to the holding cord using **DOUBLE HALF HITCH KNOTS**. Tie each knot individually onto the holding cord (It may be easier to secure the holding cord on both ends).

5. Once secured, take the first section of white cord (totaling eight cords) and divide them into two sets of four. Use the first set of four cords and tie a **SQUARE KNOT**. Repeat with the other four cords.

6. For the next row down, take the four middle cords and make a **SQUARE KNOT**. Continue with the **ALTERNATING SQUARE KNOT** pattern until you have eleven rows.

7. Repeat Steps 5 and 6 with the other three sections of white cords.

8. Use the first section of navy cords and make a **SQUARE KNOT SINNET** long enough to meet the ends of the white cord (about 7 inches). Repeat with the other two sets of navy cord.

Fig. A

Fig. B

9. Once all seven sections of knots are completed and the ends are fairly even, lay a second 2-foot strand of white cord across all the working cords. Tie each strand of working cord onto this holding cord using **DOUBLE HALF HITCH KNOTS**. (Figs. A & B)

10. Repeat Steps 5 through 9 twice to complete two more sections of this pattern. After all forty-four working cords are secured to the last holding cord, cut the ends to match the other end of the rug. Cut the ends of each holding cord coming from the sides of the rug and seal.

11. Lay your work on the floor and enjoy the feeling of a handmade macramé rug underfoot!

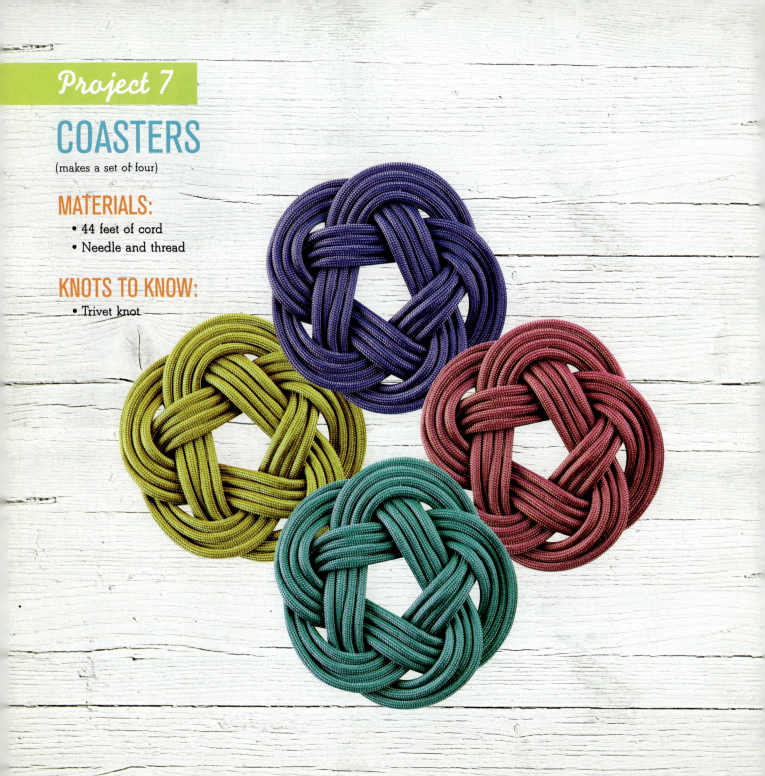

Project 7

COASTERS

(makes a set of four)

MATERIALS:
- 44 feet of cord
- Needle and thread

KNOTS TO KNOW:
- Trivet knot

INSTRUCTIONS:

1. Cut four 130-inch strands of cord, one strand for each coaster. Take one of the cords and secure the left end using pins or tape.

2. You will be making five loops, or five "sides," to make the first coaster. To make it easier to follow, the loops will be referred to as L1 (Loop 1), L2 (Loop 2), etc. Take the right end of the cord, which should have the most length, and make a loop. (This is L1.)

3. Using the same working cord, make a second loop and bring the working cord over L1. (It should resemble a pretzel at this stage.) (Fig. A)

4. Thread the working cord under the straight, beginning portion of L1 and over L2. Tighten the slack just enough to form L3. (Fig. B)

5. Thread the working cord under L1, then over, under, and over L3. (Fig. C)

6. Pull in any slack, leaving enough to form L4.

7. Thread the working cord under L2, and this will now form L5 and complete the five loops. (Fig. D)

8. Repeat Steps 2 through 7 three times, totaling four passes. Once you have finished your fourth pass, be sure both ends of the cord are underneath the coaster.

9. Cut the ends and use a needle to thread a string through the two ends to keep them together and from letting the coaster come unraveled.

10. Repeat Steps 2 through 10 to create three more coasters.

Fig. A

Fig. B

Fig. C

Fig. D

SHELF

MATERIALS:

- 12-by-5-½-by-¾ inches piece of wood
- Drill
- Sander
- Stain or paint (optional)

FOR THE MACRAMÉ:

- 35 feet of cord
- Metal ring
- 8 beads (should be large enough to accommodate the strands of cord going through each bead)

KNOTS TO KNOW:

- Gathering knot
- Spiral knot
- Overhand knot

Customize your shelf even more by using different stains and/or different colored cords to fit a variety of décors. Or make a two- or even three-tier shelf by starting with longer cords, and secure another piece of wood with additional knots.

INSTRUCTIONS:

Preparing the wood:

- If you do not have the proper tools to cut your own wood at home, have a piece cut for you at a home improvement store.

- Drill a hole into each corner of the wood. (Each hole should be just large enough for four strands of cord to fit through.)

- Sand the wood and wipe away any sawdust.

- You can leave the wood as is, or stain or paint any color you wish. Note: Be sure the wood is dry before threading through the macramé portion of this project.

1. Cut four 40-inch strands of cord and four 65-inch strands of cord.

2. Thread all cords through the metal ring, making sure that the cord is centered through it.

3. Tie a **GATHERING KNOT** around all sixteen cords. Cut and seal.

4. Divide the cords into four groups of four. Make sure each group is made up of two longer cords and two shorter cords.

5. Take the first group of four and choose the two longer pieces as your working cords.

6. Use the working cords to make a **SPIRAL KNOT SINNET** until you have about 13 inches completed.

7. Thread all four strands of cord through a bead. (Fig. A)

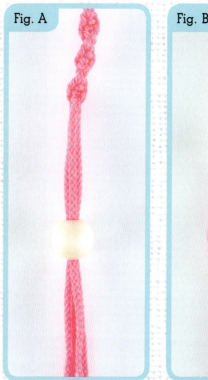
Fig. A

Fig. B

8. Tie an **OVERHAND KNOT** to secure the bead (Fig. B)

9. Repeat Steps 5 through 8 with the remaining three groups of cord.

10. Thread each set of cords through one hole in the wood.

11. Thread each set of cords through a second bead below the shelf and tie an **OVERHAND KNOT** to secure. Depending on the type of cord you choose, you may want to tie a second overhand knot to make it more secure.

12. Cut the cord tassels or leave them hanging.

OWL

MATERIALS:

- 46 feet of cord
- One 8-inch wooden dowel
- Hook or swivel
- 2 round beads
- 1 smaller bead
- Fabric dye

KNOTS TO KNOW:

- Lark's head knot
- Square knot
- Alternating square knot
- Double half hitch knot
- Gathering double half hitch knot

INSTRUCTIONS:

1. Cut nine 60-inch strands of cord and one 12-inch strand of cord.

2. Connect the ends of the 12-inch cord with an **OVERHAND KNOT** and hang on a hook or swivel.

3. Fold eight of the 60-inch cords in half and tie onto the hanging cord using **LARK'S HEAD KNOTS**.

4. Connect two sets of cord using a **SQUARE KNOT**. Continue to fill the first row with square knots, making a total of four rows.

5. Make three more rows of **ALTERNATING SQUARE KNOTS**, tying one less knot per row. You will have four knots in the first row, then three in the second, two in the third, and one in the fourth row.

6. Using the outer left cord as your holding cord, take the cord next to it and tie it onto the holding cord using a **DOUBLE HALF HITCH KNOT**. Repeat with each cord until you reach the middle. The holding cord should be going down at an angle, along the edges of the square knots. (Fig. A)

7. Repeat Step 6 using the outer right cord as your holding cord. (Figs. B & C)

8. Thread a bead through the fourth cord on each side. (These will be your owl's eyes.)

9. On a working board or, if against a wall, by taping the ends to the wall, secure one 60-inch strand of cord so that it is horizontal with your owl. This will be your holding cord. Place it just below the owl's eyes.

Fig. A

Fig. B

Fig. C

Fig. D

Fig. E

10. Starting on the left side, take the working cords (the cords on your owl) and using a **DOUBLE HALF HITCH KNOT,** tie them onto the holding cord.

11. Once you have reached the center, string a smaller bead onto the holding cord and put into place. (This will be your owl's beak.)

12. Using the outer right cord, tie **DOUBLE HALF HITCH KNOTS** onto the holding cord until you have reached the center.

13. Use the far right cord on the left section of your owl as your new holding cord and bring it across the owl at a slight downward angle and tie **DOUBLE HALF HITCH KNOTS** onto it using the working cords. (Figs. D & E)

14. Repeat Step 13 three more times on the left side of the owl.

15. Repeat Step 13 on the right side of the owl, but using the inner left cord. Repeat this step three more times on the right side of the owl.

16. Use the far right cord on the left section of your owl as the holding cord to continue another set of double half hitch knots. However, this time, it will be a **GATHERING DOUBLE HALF HITCH KNOT.**

17. Tie a **DOUBLE HALF HITCH KNOT** onto the holding cord with the cord directly next to it. Instead of dropping it and going to the next cord, hold onto it and take the next cord in your hand as well. You will have two working cords in your hands. Tie a **DOUBLE HALF HITCH KNOT** with both cords. Keep adding a cord as you go, gathering them up and tying the double half hitch knots until you are at the end. Repeat on the right side.

18. Separate three strands of cord on the left side of your owl. Bring these cords down, and up and over your dowel, with the cords hanging down behind it.

19. Repeat Step 18 on the right side. (These will be your owl's feet.)

20. Gather all of your cords together under the dowel. Use one cord from the gathered bunch and use it as your working cord. Tie four **DOUBLE HALF HITCH KNOTS** vertically around the gathered bunch of cords directly below the dowel to hold it in place. Cut the ends to your desired length. (The ends are your owl's tail.)

21. Follow the directions to prepare your chosen fabric dye. Dip the tail into the dye for the recommended amount of time.

Project 10

SHOULDER BAG

MATERIALS:
- 410 feet of cord
- Fabric glue

KNOTS TO KNOW:
- Square knot sinnet
- Lark's head knot
- Square knot
- Alternating square knot
- Double half hitch knot
- Overhand knot

INSTRUCTIONS:

For the strap:

1. Cut two 15-foot and two 8-foot strands of cord.

2. Secure all four strands with the longer cords on the outside as the working cords and the shorter cords on the inside as the holding cords. (Fig. A)

3. Tie a **SQUARE KNOT SINNET** 20 inches long. Leave 2 inches of loose cord on each end of the strap. (Fig. B)

For the bag:

1. Cut forty 9-foot and one 4-foot strand.

2. Lay out the 4-foot strand of cord. You may want to secure the ends of this holding cord.

3. Fold a strand of the 9-foot cord in half and tie onto the 4-foot holding cord using a **LARK'S HEAD KNOT**.

4. Repeat with the other thirty-nine strands of cord. Leave about 1 inch of space between the twenty and twenty-first cords. One side of the strap will be placed here. This will also separate the two sides of the bag.

5. Focus on one side of the bag first. Start at the top and tie a row of ten **SQUARE KNOTS**. Continue making **ALTERNATING SQUARE KNOTS** for each row, tying one less knot per row. There will be a row of ten, then nine, eight and so on, until you have a row of just one square knot. It should form an upside down triangle. (Fig. C)

6. Take the top left cord and bring it down horizontally, following the left side of the pattern. (This is your holding cord.)

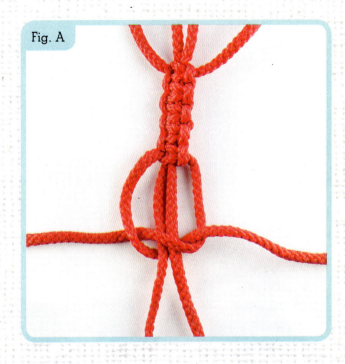

Fig. A

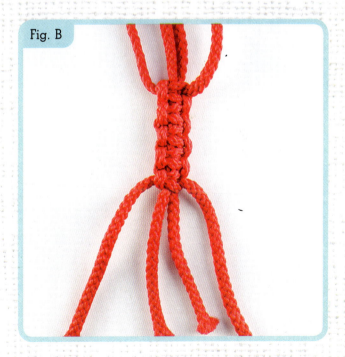

Fig. B

Fig. C

Fig. D

Fig. E

Fig. F

Fig. G

Fig. H

7. Tie a **DOUBLE HALF HITCH KNOT** onto the holding cord using the cord next to it. Continue with each additional cord until you have reached the middle.

8. Repeat Step 7 on the opposite side, using the top right cord and bringing it down the right side of the pattern. (Figs. D & E)

9. Repeat Steps 5 through 8 for the bag's other side.

10. Now, focus on the area between the two triangles, where one end of the bag strap will be placed. Starting at the top, use two cords from the left side and two from the right to make a **SQUARE KNOT**. (Figs. F–H)

11. For the next row down, use the two right cords of the square knot you just made, and two more cords from the right triangle and make a **SQUARE KNOT**. Use the two left cords of the first square knot and two more cords from the left triangle and make another **SQUARE KNOT**. Continue this alternating square knot pattern, keeping the knots spaced about ½-inch apart until you have ten rows of alternating square knots. (Figs. I & J)

12. Flip the bag over, lay out and bring the ends together, folding over the middle. (Figs. K & L)

13. Repeat Steps 10 and 11 to connect the two ends of the bag together. Keep the knotwork on this side of the bag fairly even with the knots of the other side of the bag. (Figs. M & N)

14. Once the sides are connected, place the bag so one side is facing up. Use the two middle cords to start forming the bottom of the bag. These will be your holding cords in the next step.

15. Bring the right holding cord over the left side of the bag, over and across the working cords horizontally. Tie each cord onto this holding cord using **DOUBLE HALF HITCH KNOTS**. Repeat on the other side by bringing the left holding cord over and across the right working cords.

16. Flip the bag over and repeat Steps 14 and 15.

17. Turn the bag inside out. A cord from the left side and a cord from the right side will be considered a set. Tie each set of cords together using an **OVERHAND KNOT**, starting from one side of the bag and making your way to the end of the other. Be sure to tighten the knots as you go. This will connect the sides and create the bottom of the bag.

18. Cut and seal the loose ends of the tied cords. Depending on the type of cord or material being used, you may wish to put a drop of fabric glue on each set of tied cords to ensure they stay together. Make sure the glue is dry before moving on to the next step.

19. Flip the bag right side out. Use the cords from one end of the strap and tie it onto the holding cord on the space you made in the beginning on top of the bag using **DOUBLE HALF HITCH KNOTS**. Cut and seal the ends with fabric glue.

20. The other end will have longer, loose cords that came together once you connected the sides of the bag. Overlap these two cords and tie the other end of the strap onto both of these cords using **DOUBLE HALF HITCH KNOTS**. Cut and seal once again.

Fig. I

Fig. J

Fig. K

Fig. L

Fig. M

Fig. N

Justine Vasquez is a content marketer who has always had a flair for anything crafty. When she is not working or making new macramé pieces, she is finding new, exciting places to take her boys, baking, and drinking a lot of coffee.